PUBLISHED by PARABLES
Earthly Stories with a Heavenly Meaning

Mike Kelley

THE WINDOWS OF LIFE

By

MIKE KELLEY

PUBLISHED by PARABLES
Earthly Stories with a Heavenly Meaning

Mike Kelley

The Windows Of Life
Mike Kelley

Published By Parables
March, 2022

All Rights Reserved. No part of this book may be reproduced or utilized in any form or by any means, electronic or mechanical, including photocopying, recording, or by any information storage and retrieval system, without permission in writing from the author.

Printed in the United States of America

Readers should be aware that Internet Web sites offered as citations and/or sources for further information may have been changed or disappeared between the time this was written and the time it is read.

The Windows Of Life
By
Mike Kelley

Earthly Stories with a Heavenly Meaning

Mike Kelley

THE WINDOWS OF LIFE

A Christian Reflection

Mike Kelley

To the pages come ink

From that ink comes words

The words inspired of God

I pray that you find his love within

Stories

Quotes

Poems

Prose

Thoughts

And Prayers

This book is dedicated to the support and love of my wife, Susan.

She the hand that holds me on course

Through the storms, my anchor

The light in my window of life

She is God' meaning of love

My blessing

The Windows of Life

Looking out the windows of life

It is my prayer

To see beyond my own reflection

Mike Kelley

Mike Kelley

Just Off Yankee Station

Dark skies loomed with the horizon hidden

The call came, the C-1A was in the landing pattern

This was the aircraft that brought in the mail

With the holidays falling this brought warm feelings

It would be several hours till the mail would be sorted

Yet, just knowing brought hopes

The ship was in a wide circle within the Red China Sea

This was off the coast of Vietnam

No one wanted to be here, yet here we were

Christmas Eve, a world away from home

An aircraft carrier with thousands of men

Our squadron awaited in the ready room

Awaiting mail, words from loved ones

Then came the word, "Mail Call"

Waiting as names were called

Smith, Lewis, Davis, Arnold, Foster

Then the last name called

I was never so homesick in my life

No mail, no card, nothing with my name

Others sat and read their letters

Some with boxes of homemade goodies

I held to a cup of coffee black, but could not swallow

At that moment I wanted to be alone

Away from those happy faces

There are few places on an aircraft carrier for solitude

Then finding the fantail deck there I stood

Rain falling and a mist being lifted from the ship's movements

Nothing to see just darkness

I didn't cry, although my heart was broken

No one wrote, I felt forgotten

I am not sure how long I stood there

The damp air only added to my dark thoughts

Then the call came over the ships PA

Our squadron to report to the ready room

I mustered my best face, and reported as called

There we were thirty-two men

Our squadron leader called us together

We sat knowing we were not scheduled for flights

The Windows Of Life

Yet, there always loomed a chance we might be called anyway

Our commander called us together to celebrate, he said

To celebrate Christmas Eve together

Then in an effort to raise morale he had a plan

We, each one was to tell of our best Christmas remembered

He started it off with a story as a child and that first bike

The stories went on and in them something unfolded

Each one brought us together in a different way

Each name on our uniforms became a person

We laughed together, and cried too

We became a family that night not fighting men

Then my turn came, and I told my story

It was a story that now I have written

I tell it each Christmas as it holds me so close

It holds me to my Kentucky roots

I call it "Grandma's Bible"

Once I looked through my grandma's bible and as a child was amazed at what I found

There were pressed between the pages treasures she kept close to her heart, and in her own way close to God

There were flowers from special events of joy and flowers from the passing of loved ones

There were newspaper clips of history changing, and an anniversary card from my grandpa signed with love

There were notes written from verse to verse, and a letter or two from family away

There were lines underlined in color with special dates written in

There were colored pictures of the life of Christ, and a cross made of lace

There were pages worn in her bible some stained with tears of hurt and joy

There were so many things to see, but the one that meant the most to me came on Christmas Eve

It was a cold winter in Kentucky and our old coal stoves bottom had just burned out, so we went to our grandparent's house till a new heat stove could be installed.

It was just a few days before Christmas, and this made things extra special for me as a child.

The Windows Of Life

It was on this visit that I found grandma's bible on the table beside the chair where she would sit, and the treasures within.

Grandma smiled as she called my name then came over and sat beside me, and without a word turned the pages to the second chapter of Luke and began to read to me.

Through her eyes that Christmas Eve I saw Mary and Joseph and could hear a donkey's feet on the journey to Bethlehem.

There was a great crowd of people and no place to stay in that city.

Mary was soon to be the mother of Jesus and with Joseph they came upon a stable to stay.

I could smell the hay and see the other animals in the stable.

Grandma's face was aglow while telling of Jesus and his birth.

She made me to understand as she moved my fingers over the lines that there was a great star, shepherds, and angels.

With her voice I heard "Glory to God in the highest and on earth peace, goodwill to men."

After reading with arms around me I was made to understand why Jesus was born, and tears fell from her eyes while speaking, all treasures have a price.

She closed her bible and placed her hand over mine on top of that holy book, closed her eyes, and spoke to God with me in her lap.

I guess if I think back to that time, we would be considered poor, but I, well I, found a real treasure in grandma's bible.

After telling my story some men sat quietly, some with a hint of a tear, I guess they too recalled their grandma's bibles and the treasures they might have held.

It was aboard the USS. Independence I found my beat-up typewriter and typed out the story. The original copy lost, but the memory not. That was my story of the best Christmas ever.

Our squadron came back home a bit battle worn and tired

We were given medals for our actions, The National Defense Service Medal with Bronze Star, Viet Nam Service Medal with Attachment, Republic of Viet Nam Campaign Medal with Device, and the Navy Unit Commendation

All that might mean something to others, but it was the memory of grandma's bible and its story told one Christmas Eve long ago I treasure most.

The Windows Of Life

The Prodigal

Rain was falling as he boarded the Greyhound
This trip too long in coming
Daylight just a mist beyond the window
Leaving town on a long-delayed trip
One he had promised to make so many times
Something always happened it seemed
The old cowboy sat in thought
Now he fell one too many times
His horse long gone, and old dog too
Boots once shined now scared with age
Where had time gone?
I 'am coming home he wrote in a letter
A letter never mailed
The rodeo called, just one more ride
Calendars turned, as months turned to years
Now the years to a lifetime of lost dreams
The bus arrived at Cincinnati as others boarded
People excited, happy faces, for the trip ahead
Seats filled as a young lady sat beside him
She smiled as he put a finger to his worn cowboy hat
It was a hello without words
They sat quictly as the bus moved out of town
The rain had grown cold and turned to sleet
Yet the seasoned driver moved safely along
He dosed with his head to the window glass
Just the feeling of cold to his head
Then came the dreams of home

He awoke as the bus slowed
Then came to a stop
The sleet had changed to snow
Flashing lights ahead as the highway was blocked
A truck and trailer lay across the roadway
Then the young lady bowed her head and whispered a prayer
Her words came softly
Like an angel talking to God
He listened and felt her plea for an unknown soul
Then she looked up and into his face
He saw a glow about her something warm
"Do you pray she asked?"
"Someone might be hurt a word could help"
The Cowboy had prayed many times in his life
Each time seemed to be for himself
For a safe ride, or to get beyond a broken bone
Her face shown him honesty as he removed his hat
Bowed his head and he lifted a prayer
"Hello God, it's me again
Lifting words for the driver that has fallen
Hold him in your hands
Give him a path home to family and loved ones"
As his words lifted, he felt a touch of his hand
She said not a word
Then a Trooper came to the bus
Told the driver that the road would be clear soon
Then told how a paramedic said the driver had passed
And was making way to pull him from the wreckage
Then a light shined from inside around him

The Windows Of Life

And the driver was now alive
It was something he couldn't explain
The young lady turned to the cowboy
"It must have been a prayer that saved him"
Then tears fell as they both knew its power
"My name is Ruth" she spoke, and he said, "Pleased to know you"
He didn't give his name it just didn't fit.
Soon the road was cleared, and the bus again was heading south
Snow fell painting the landscape in pure white
The lights of Louisville were bright and colorful as they arrived
Christmas in the air, this eve.
He gathered his worn traveling bag
Then Ruth touched his arm and said "Merry Christmas, Mike"
He looked at her puzzled, he had not given his name
Then she was gone just vanished it seemed
Looking around but no sight of her anywhere
He made his way from the station to the sidewalk
There he stood looking up at the snow falling
It was on this very sidewalk he had left home
Things had changed over the years
He too had changed
There was no one to meet him
He took a taxi down Preston Street
Then got out at a place called, Evergreen
Paid the taxi and climbed over the fence
It was the resting place of the departed
Stone by stone he walked

Mike Kelley

Then he came to the place he was looking for
It was a stone that held their names
Etched to their life and deaths
He sat in the snow as warm tears fell
He, spoke of sorrows and his failures
Too late to change things
Too late to start over, his days too passing
Then as he reached out holding the cold stone
A voice came to him, "Merry Christmas, Mike"
Turning around there she stood, Ruth
"Tonight, your prayer saved one life and now your will be rewarded with a new tomorrow"
Looking up Ruth lifted away in the falling snow
Looking around there were no footprints where she stood
There was only an echo of her soft voice in his mind
Pushing his face in the cold snow he felt a peace as never before
Then lifting his head up there stood a child calling out to him
"Daddy, are you OK, you fell in the snow"
Things changed he was a young man again
Standing in the yard beside a snowman his son built
Home, his home
His life had changed
Standing up brushing off the snow there she was
Ruth holding a cup of hot coco and saying,
Merry Christmas, Mike.
The End,
Or maybe the new beginning.

The Little Dog of Bethlehem
(The Legend)

As legends are told of a time in history this one too is such a story. It is about a dog with no name, just a street dog in the dusty city of Bethlehem in the days of Caesar Augustus, and Herod the King. Is it true or fiction, as are most legends are a bit of both maybe?

The city was full with people and families, carts and donkeys. There was much noise about and shouting about a taxation that had to be paid.

This made it hard for a little dog one that had to stay away from the mainstream of people who would just assume kick him as not. So, he had to find a place to stay away from the crowds.

Working his way around the city staying to the shadows he came upon a stable and hid among the hay. Still the voices came as people were in the streets and talking loudly.

Then came the stable keeper through the door and directed a donkey with a woman and another man guiding the animal. It was clear she would be having a baby soon and the words exchanged was there was no other place for them to stay, so the stableman allowed them a place to rest as the baby was coming. And so, it was the child was born and wrapped in swaddling clothes and placed in the manger as a crib.

The little dog watched with wide eyes while hiding in the shadows. There was a warm glow when the child was born something special. There was something more as soon shepherds came talking of angels and a multitude of the heavenly host praising God and saying, "Glory to God in the highest, and on earth peace among men with whom he is pleased!". Then they came to see this child and there they found Mary and Joseph and the child that the angels had spoken of.

Then came three wise men from the East, following a star that shown over them till it came to rest over the place where the child was. They rejoiced exceedingly with great joy and came to worship him this baby, bringing gifts of riches of gold, frankincense and myrrh.

Then as the night came later and everyone had settled in the little dog came to see this child. He was asleep and so full of peace. The little dog thought he too must bring a gift to the child, but what is it that he might give.

Venturing out he went to the outer gates and into the fields and there he saw the star shining above, the sign of something very special of which the wise men spoke. As he looked the light from the star sent down light to the ground and he saw a bush with thorns and a flower in bloom. This is what I should take this fragrant flower to the baby. He chewed the stem and brought it and lay it at the foot of the child and started to back away when the baby opened his eyes and didn't cry but looked on with a wonderful brightness within. Moving closer to the child it moved a hand then a finger and touched the little dogs' eyes. Something happened, it changed the dog and from that point on all the dogs on earth were blessed with unconditional love.

Then the man Joseph awoke the earthly father saw the rose and handed it to his wife Mary and said, I love you and from that point on the rose has been the symbol of love exchanged throughout the world.

That is the legend as it is, and who among us knows if there was a little dog for sure? I do see however, unconditional love in the eyes of the dogs everywhere, just looking it could be so, is the look that was exchanged in the stable there? and the rose oh, the rose how did it get chosen as love exchanged?

When you hear the song, "Away in the Manger" this year, you might just see in your mind a little dog with a rose in its mouth bringing a gift of love to the savior of the world, Emmanuel (God with us).

Merry Christmas, and may you exchange love, and unconditional love, in this season as we worship the birth of a child in a stable in Bethlehem. Jesus the one who first brought that unconditional love to mankind and opened the door for eternal life.

Mike Kelley

The Dying Season

Hello God, It's Me Again

Lifting a prayer with heavy grief

This past year has been one of great pain in this world

One where lives have been altered with loss

The world has counted it numbers

[So] has the book of life

[Sp]irits of mother and fathers

[Sp]irits of brothers and sisters

[Sp]irits of friends and neighbors

[Sp]irits lifted away

[Fr]om your holy word we read

[A] time to be born and a time to die

[Th]is is the journey of us all

[Fr]om the cradle to the grave

[Yo]u know of us in this journey

[W]e are yours in your hand

[W]e pray with grief, so much it seems to fall

[No]w with the evil winds that have come

[Li]ves lifted away in the dark hours of night

Mike Kelley

Families torn and tears shed

We are parted with unknown days of life

Our time is yours, and in your hand

In remembrance of the birth of your son Jesus

We will not turn away

We that take our breath even in grief will celebrate

There is a purpose

A time to be born and a time to die

As we stumble and fall, as we lift our prayers

We will not turn away

This old world has got might evil

Satin has found a place to play

Yet we can do something about it

As we lift our voice in prayer

Yes, we cry with the losses as the numbers grow

Yet, God we open our eyes to you

Looking for our purpose in this life

Looking to be a hand that reaches beyond our door

To touch others that feel that pain of loss

To listen to their voices and be in return a comforter

To be Christian when the going is up a rough mountain

The Windows Of Life

ive us strength to fight the power of Satin

    Death is not the end, just a change in direction

    We give our lives to you to be a vessel of love

    Use us in this dark hour for so many

    Let us be your hands

    Let us do as you so direct

    This is my prayer, and a prayer that others might pray

    Give us your ear, as we reach to your hand

    If this dying season be of us also

    Let our hearts reach out to the living

    As did Jesus from the cross

    A-Men

Mike Kelley

Winter Cold

Winds cast snow to the air and upon the limbs

Ice grips to the fences

Fields hold a carpet of white

Grey looms in heavy clouds of winter

Tis a season of winter cold

Ice forms in the ponds

Streams slow in their travel over frosty borders

The world in slumber

Yet not all of nature is still

Whispers heard from a bird's call

Crisp sound echoes from a branch

Lost to man it lifts a prayer

Even nature has learned of God

The God that gives to the needs such as this

The same God that holds us in winter cold

Winters cold grip is of the earth's seasons

Oh, that we were as the little bird

That we lift a prayer of faith in life's storms

That our eyes see beyond the grey to find light

Mike Kelley

Winter is cold as the trials of the world

We huddle for warmth

When it is just a prayer away

Lift our voice as a bird's call

For over us all is warmth

Reach out and embrace that God that uphold nature

Let the dark winds blow

Let the clouds be full

Let your feet crunch the snow

As God makes a path

Even in winter cold

Cowboy Christmas Eve

Off the trail towards a place called home

To be around folks one loves

Too long gone with dreams that fail

Married to a horse and old dog

Riding ranges of endless land

Years have passed all too quickly

Winter can be bitter with its breath

Campfires fight but lose to keep one warm

The last few miles come with the ringing of bells

The church in celebration of Christmas

Sitting the saddle now with a quicken pace

To join with mom and dad

Music lifts over the snow

Sweet songs of the birth of Jesus

Away in a manger comes to him with tears

Folks turn and look with smiles

The desperado came home

Moving down the aisle mom cries in welcome

Dad pulls him in with a hug

Tonight, he will sleep under a warm quilt

He will reflect on new tomorrows

Old yesterday's lay broken in a troubled mind

He is down to four round gold coins

And this is his offering to God

No matter he knows the love of money makes a fool

Holding on to a worn song book he sings

Silent Night, with a voice just above a whisper

Standing there he feels someone move to his side

Her voice rings like an angel

It is Holly, the girl he left behind

She smiles as if it were yesterday when they were in their youth

He touches her hand lightly

She takes it with a warm squeeze

Maybe it is not too late

Maybe his travels have brought him where he needs to be

He closes his eyes to lift a silent prayer

When he opens again everything is gone

The Windows Of Life

The Church, mom, dad, and Holly

He is outside in the cold snow of winter

It is Christmas Eve

He packs up all his shabby belongings and rides out

Over the crest of the mountains down towards home

Stars break through the darkness as he pushes on

Riding now with purpose

Riding with hope

He will be home come Christmas morning

His prayer lifted that as moonlight fell over the trail

In the late hours long past midnight he sees the light

The candle in the window flickered

This Christmas Eve has brought him home

Then a voice came with the winds

As he listened to God

"Ascribe to the Lord of families of the peoples, ascribe to the Lord glory and strength."

He entered his home with rejoicing and celebration

Warm tears around the fire of reunion

Mom read the story of Christ and his birth

They prayed together and slept the sleep of peace

Mike Kelley

He awoke as the snow had lifted away

Then to the little church to welcome in Christmas

Then just as in his trail dream, Holly, held to his hand

The cowboy was home.

Just a cowboy Christmas Eve to remember

It is now my prayer that all the cowboys make it home

To give up old dreams and find new trails

To find the love of God and family

To celebrate the wonders   A-Men

The Windows Of Life

Hands Reach Out with A Pencil

Scratching marks across endless pages

Words crashing to others

Books and binders hold thousands

Some God gives wings to

He the master of subjects

In his call I hold the pencil

I push on to another page

Another sheet fills with thoughts

Sometimes a parable

Sometimes a prayer

Sometimes just words to color tomorrow

Darkness even has a purpose to my God

Not a place to hide in the shadows

A place to think beyond, with a prayer through the clouds

Some words fall like flowers of his beauty

Some to songs to sing

I am the holder of the pencil

God is the hand that moves the words

Mike Kelley

The Windows Of Life

Front Row Seats

Some years ago, my son Shane and I went to a Reds Game

We had some great seats, albeit not in the front row

I have never been much of a front row guy

We could almost smell their popcorn however

The closer you get to the front row things change

You feel the excitement, the energy at its greatest

The Reds lost that day, and there was a fight on the field

Both teams emptied the benches

It was a brush-back pitch that started the action

Well tonight I am thinking of other front row seats

The Kentucky Derby, now to have a front row seat there, wow

My older brother Don and I were serving as honor guards

We were just behind the fence on the track

We could see over to the other side

The side where the Front row people sat

Mike Kelley

John Wayne, Dean Martin, the Governor of Kentucky

Oh, we had the best place in the Derby to be

As it turned out I passed out in the hot sun

My brother drug me to first aid

We missed the greatest race of the year!

In school I never wanted to be front row

I was the kid that always talked in class

Tonight, it is other front rows I am thinking of

Not the front row in the airplane

Nor the front row at a concert

Not the front row at some sports event

It is the front row that took away a great friend

Front row combat, Vietnam

Other front rows might stand out in thought

Sunday 1941 at Pearl Harbor

Hiroshima, Nagasaki, at ground zero

Maybe the trains to Stalingrad

Or maybe front row street level at the Worlds Trade Center

We find at times front row is not where we want to be at all

The Windows Of Life

Looking around at life God has a front row to it all

He sees us at our best and worst

Sees even deeper that our front row selves

He sees the outward display we try to paint of ourselves

But he also knows our hearts and the hidden self-inside

Someday our front row events will all come to an end

Those expensive tickets we might buy lost

I do want to be on that front row when Christ returns

I don't need a program

I don't need popcorn

I just need to be there when the saints come marching in.

Mike Kelley

Christmas Rains Came to Cincinnati

Over the seven hills

Across the city

Down to the river

Rain came, a washing rain

Like a baptism

What better a day for such?

This day, a birthday for Jesus

Let the rains fall

Let us rejoice as we are washed clean

We can celebrate the birth of Christ

With a new birth within ourselves

Mike Kelley

Once Upon A Time, Or In The Beginning.

I have spent so much of my life with a pencil in hand scratching across anything that was blank to express myself in some way, good and bad. I however realize that when a story stars off, "Once upon a time" it is usually a made-up tale for children. You might take note that the bible doesn't start off "Once up a time" it starts off with, "In the beginning" yet some might look upon it as a story only for Christians, the odd people that follow its words for knowledge and instruction. Once upon a time might have a place but if the bible started off as such the story would still leads us through the travels of mankind, its pitfalls, and the hope for something beyond. It would tell of a child born in a manger and a father in heaven. It would tell us a story that is filled with poetry, parables, an attitude, we call the "Be attitudes" it is not a fairy tale it is a story of history, a story of love, a story of loss, a story of forgiveness, a story that truly was, In the beginning, and tells us to decide for ourselves its ending. It is not how it begins that counts the ending is in all our hands, and souls.

The Windows Of Life

Looking Back

As this year finds its final day

It is within us to look back at where we have been

Maybe a rearview mirror of a road passed

A bridge not crossed

The past is the dust of yesterday

Cast off what could have been

And be more in the days ahead

Be

Awake in your mind
Wise in spirit
Happy in your heart
Take time to understand
Make sound judgments
Be ready, not risky
Move in a forward direction
Avoid fools and folly
Stand up for something
Seek love and the human spirit
Become yourself and like it
Live life and be free within your soul
See God and find peace
Be

Looking back to time fading, let it go

Mike Kelley

Looking today, now be as God would have you be

Now not a Happy New Year I wish

I wish you a Happy New Life

My Garden Tree

There is a tree in my garden

It's not so very tall

And slightly shades the moonlight

From the ground where it might fall

A warm breeze passes gently through

As the limbs whisper a call

It's the Holy breath of Heaven

God gives freely to us all

There is a tree in my garden

Where I go to pray

As even nightbirds listen

Mike Kelley

For the voice of my Lord, what he will
Say

Like angels all around me

Leaves flicker in the twilight of day

Singing songs of his returning

Time now, Jesus is on his way

There is a tree in my garden

And there was one at Calvary too

My Saviors blood was shed upon it

This with love for me and you

The wood, it held the weight

Of God's only begotten son

For six hours in the time of man

The Windows Of Life

The tree and he were one

Now, there is no tree at Calvary

Nor one in my garden man can see

It's with my faith in the believing

A tree of life grows for all eternally

Do you have a tree in your garden?

This is not just a vision for me

I have a tree in my garden

It's Jesus, the tree of life

That is the tree I see

Do you have a tree in your garden?

Mike Kelley

Watch Night

When I was a young man, I was called of God
It was a New Year's Eve
The Minister of a little Church prayed with me
Then asked me to deliver a sermon for Watch Night
Watch night was looking ahead to the new year
Looking ahead to what might be in life
The passage I was given
It was from Ecclesiastes the third chapter
Ecclesiastes (The Preacher) it means

I was on a path then to become a preacher
To share the love of God
I recall that night, I was a seventeen-year-old youth
The subject was so bold
Reading and rereading the words I felt them
They spoke to me of adventure
Of challenges, and of thought
Thing to put in perspective
I stood in front of the people of that little church
There were people I knew well in attendance

The Windows Of Life

My family was there, even grandparents came

It was a night that before I spoke one word

Before all, God took control

I had notes to cover the text

Notes to point to the future ahead

A new year coming

The notes lay beside my bible

Next to Ecclesiastes chapter three

Yet my words and notes were not used

A prayer was lifted

I gave myself to God to speak

Then what was said was not of me

It came from him

Notes lay never followed

The little light at the pulpit could have been off

For it was a moment of complete trust that preached that night

It was not a night about me

It was a night in God's hands, and words

I never went on to become the Preacher

Oh, I was called, but I let the world get in the way

Yet later God called me to a different service

I had to seek and lose, to cast away, to weep, and find a war to find the peace that was to be.

God didn't call of me to preach, but to be a hand to his words

I have a regret in this new year

One spoken of in a book called The River Cries

It was a book of everything under the sun

Written to inspire the minds and heart

To touch lives as a band of travelers came together

Searching for what was ahead

What was around that next bend in the river

To feel the past event and taste the fruit of adventure

To touch on a time to be born and die

A voice came from beyond to solve a wrong

It also covered a time to heal a broken life

One touched in a poem of a purple frog

The book was a regret not because its failure to sell

I was never looking for riches

I was reaching in vanity of self

Albeit of a Christian nature it was not fully from God

The Windows Of Life

It was a lesson learned through regret

The new year has come, and another time to review our lives

Be it on a trip down a river, or just going nowhere

It is a time to give thought to our past and maybe

Just maybe, cast off a few things that slow us down

To leave old baggage behind

Maybe a time to look ahead not behind

Leave the regrets and let the river cry

God will pick you up, it is just a prayer away

No regrets now, just Happy New Year

Journals

Through the years of journals

Pages hold me in thought

Sometimes a wild story

Sometimes thoughts of love

Poems that come in the night

Sketches at times

Stamps from foreign places

Photo pasted to the page with word of expression

Quotes

Words written with tears

Prayers of expression

Thoughts in ink, pencil, or type

Measurements of something to build

Journals that reflect me

Some humor

Some hurt

Words that call me to write

Words that should have been said

The valentine words from my heart

The Windows Of Life

Pages also in life that changes

Now, beside my desk one sits awaiting words

Others all about the home

Journals that share me in travels

Words sometimes of my youth

Words that cry with age

Thoughts etched of loved ones

Memories of lost loves

Journals become filled with emotions

Pages that cover years in record

When completed they become just as loved

Placed in safe keeping

They become a mirror with I the reflection

It is my place of secret words

Why do I keep Journals?

It is the music I play

The art I paint

A voice that whispers

Words to a Greater Spirit

It is life to me

My journals and my bibles hold me

Mike Kelley

Both are holy things to my soul

And maybe my final eulogy

Spring Will Come Again

I was saddened when I saw the trees standing stripped against a winter's sky

Today they seemed to shiver with a chill in the air

Having lost their beauty from the spring to the fall

Standing almost like a monument of something lost, something strong and tall

Looking into its shape now I see a home in a hollow of branches

A family of squirrels finding protection for winter so close to the heart of the tree itself

Trees reach out with love for nature around, and provide a haven against the elements to others in God's Kingdom

Reaching out at a time when they have little else to offer, they offer their best, their all

Maybe we could learn from trees to reach out and hold on to something with love as bitter winds of life blow through our branches

Yes, hold on, spring will come again

Dark Night Ink

Lifting a pen

After a moment of prayer

Black ink flows to the page

I am amazed as words take shape

More amazed at what they say

The words of my sins

One by one they fill the page

Then another page and on and on

It haunts me all the sins lined up

Seems the evil of the world has been in me

Parts of me so dark exposed to the pages

It brings tears of confession of my failings

It brings a burning hurt to have wasted so much

One never starts out to be as black as the ink

Darkly displayed in the eyes of the world

Yet, I have been

Then as I was writing along the ink changed

It became a red ink

The Windows Of Life

No, not ink at all

It was written in blood

Then I looked back over the pages

All the black sins in black ink were gone

The blood released me and made me free

Need I tell you whose blood that was

Need I paint it to your life

The first letter of John 1-7, 8, 9

If we walk in the light, as he is in the light we have fellowship with one another, and the blood of Jesus his Son cleanses us from all sin. If we say we have no sin we deceive ourselves and the truth is not in us, if we confess our sins, he is faithful and just, and will forgive our sins and cleanse us from all unrighteousness.

No, I need not write it, it was written on a cross with a promise to all who believe.

If you're brave enough, take up the pen

Write out your sins in the black ink of life

How many pages can you fill?

How many?

Then Confess them and watch what happens

Mike Kelley

Lost in life

When comes a time of trouble

When friends cannot be found

When we forget how to pray

We slip away into hopelessness

We hear the voice inside calling us away

Curse God and die

Hello God, It's Me Again

Lifting a prayer for someone who slipped

Someone who fell

Someone who on the verge of stepping away from life

Once heard a young man's prayers

Sad words lifted he, as on the verge

Ready to step away from this life

No place to turn

His prayer was spoken

To be his last words

It was a prayer lifted to no one just spoken

"Give me not a place in life

Not a child, nor a wife

The Windows Of Life

Give me only what I earn

Let me light the fires

Let me burn

Forgive me now as on earth I fail

As my last steps are from here to hell"

He didn't take that last step

Someone saw his trouble

Someone spoke

Then together they prayed

A friend unknown reached out

God gave words of hope to a hopeless soul

Tears washed down

A life and soul were saved

This life today seems so fragile at times

People, good people dying all too soon

We have all sinned and come short of the glory of God

Yet, Lord, you send us the broken to help the broken

We who ourselves suffer from things of this world

We hang our hats on the hope and faith that you will see us through

Then when all seems so lost

Mike Kelley

You put us in a place of someone who stumbles

Someone listening not to you but the dark voice

That voice of Satin

His calling to a troubled mind

His calling to curse God and die

That is not of you

In your holy book

The 18th book of the Old Testament

A soul is troubled

He is praying words without understanding

How he who served you could be so cast down

His family broken, daughters and sons gone

A wife who turned her back

All worldly goods taken away

Even health pulling to the dust of the earth

He, a good man

His friends judge him wrongly

They feel he has sinned against you

But, even at the darkest hour you were there

He didn't know it

The Windows Of Life

Ready to die and plead his case to you

Why me?

It was such a test to his faithfulness

The sad story had an ending of change

One that God blessed the faithful one

The story holds true today as of old

We are yours to use

Give us a voice

Mode us as the clay

Have thy own way Lord

Have thy own way

You are the potter

We are the clay

Forgive us our sins

Show us the way

This is my prayer, Lord

A prayer that lifted me up when fallen

Now help me to lift up others

Not to judge, but to support

Not to turn away, but to turn to

Mike Kelley

This I pray

Of a family

Lost without the things of this life

Lost with only a hope to see a tomorrow

Do not let us pass them by

Be they beside the road in a tent

Or sleeping in a car

Or maybe a park bench

Put us in their path and use us

Lord, God take us, the clay

And have thy way

A-Men

Moon Wisdom

Moving the tides that splash across to some lost shore

The moon pulls at the waters as always before

God put his hand on that old lunar globe

There is a purpose in this, so we are told

Under the same moon we take such delight

Viewing up to its glow in the dark of night

Lovers hold hands and look upon its face

As hearts quicken at a warming pace

The moon beams dance across the shadows of night

As some dream their dreams and never capture its sight

Sadly, we let the night pass to the day

The wisdom lost, words it did not say

Oh, the moon is not as wise as God

But maybe he gives it a wink or nod

He uses the light softly to divide the dark

To shine through a window casting its mark

Mike Kelley

Time to remember the world in need of prayer

The moon has its purpose, so God put it there

The sea will rush, from the power of a moons pull

But is of God, that gives wisdom, be not a fool

The reflections are cast across the waters of life

Take peace and comfort, and away with strife

God shines brighter than the moon or sun

In the light of the moon pray that his will be done

Let the moon be as the globe of night

Let God guide us with his heavenly light

Wisdom is not of the moon, be not a fool

Be a student of God in his holy school

Study to show yourself approved onto God

Wisdom beyond that Solomon gave shod

Never stop learning even in the dark of night

Never stop learning even if by a moons lowly light

Take me to sail on the sea by the moon above

Teach me all the lessons of life, and of a Jesus love

The Windows Of Life

Give me your hand strong beyond some faint light

This my prayer now prayed, under a moon less bright

Mike Kelley

Snow lays lightly

As like onto a wedding dress

Pure and white with soft folds

Hovering over the seeds of spring

Hiding the grey skies above

As the honeymoon of nature sleeps

God smiles

Then, on that spring day as snow melts

Blossoms come, blooms unfold, and skies turn blue

There is a season for all things under the sun

Let the snow fall for to follow comes spring

He Had a Dream

Never again will he dream

But I remember as tears stream

A man who stood in the shadows of God

Who walked this earth where others feared to trod?

A man of black with a dream for us all

Sad it was in Memphis he had to fall

But he left us all with a spirit of light

A message did not end that dreadful night

Now we honor him for his vision to see

What from a dream could really be?

Mike Kelley

I was stationed at the Naval Air Technical Training Center located just outside Memphis the night of the shooting of Martin Luther King Jr. April 4th, 1968, I still feel the shock and horror of the events at the Lorain Motel and a great since of loss for a disciple of equality and peace. I however rejoice in that the "Dream Lives On" and now, so we pick up the cross. Each year I lift a prayer to honor the man and the God, he served.

Everyday Angels

The artist of old once painted angels

Floating within clouds with long flowing gowns

This may be true

But there are others I believe

Those in everyday attire

Those that bring something special

A lesson to be learned

The everyday angels

How blessed we are to live in such a world

A world of everyday angels

Listen

Can you not hear without words?

Can you not feel without touch?

Can you not know love without change?

From God comes a voice at times without words

From God comes a feel without touch

From God comes love with change

I have looked in the eyes of nature

The birds, and rabbits, and all he gives life to

To the dogs that sit at my feet

They have looked into my heart

They have spoken without a word

They have touched without a feel

They have loved as God has given

They may well be a messenger to the heart

Can you not hear without word?

Are you not listening?

The sparrow sits in the hand of God

As do we

Listen

Christmas Bells

If I could pull the ropes that ring the bells of Christmas

I would pull as hard as I could

I would want them to ring so you could hear

I would want the world to hear

I would want God in heaven to hear

If I could pull the ropes that ring the bells of Christmas
I would want peace for all

I would want health to be yours

I would want your life filled with joy

I would want you filled with hope

If I could pull the ropes that ring the bells of Christmas
I would want for nothing more.

Mike Kelley

Peace, be still

Words of Jesus to calm the waters

Peace be still

In these times of change

In a world at times out of control

We feel the darkness of the valley of death

Our prayers are lifted

To a God who listens

Beyond the horizons he sees our storms

And in faith even in the darkest hour

We feel the comfort while facing our troubles

Comfort of his hand sweeping across our lives

Comfort of his words

Peace, be still

There is a Path

There is a path through woods that lead beyond

Somewhere through trees, somewhere into life

It is but a holy place, one with footprints of God

Some have walked with prayers lifted

Others stand mute in a beauty beyond words

Each step taken leave to a discovery

Small things become noticed

A crafted handiwork of a spider's web

Stones with shape and color that holds moss with love

Mushrooms rise up from shade

Wildflowers hold out to butterfly kisses

Breezes carry a fragrance of wild onions

Sunlight filters through branches as leaves part

Sounds of water falling over rocks in a stream

Creatures of nature appear, turtles in a sunny spot

Frogs hop through long grasses into waters cool

A snake slides past without sound, yet sleek in travel

Rabbits of wild play at thickets edge

Singing birds lift songs to this day in peace

Mike Kelley

Blackberries fill vines lush with a harvest for taking

Here air comes fresh to mankind

Here the soil from which man was made

This, a path through a holy garden called Eden

Lost now in time is this path

Lost is the garden

Yet, not lost, is how to travel it

Sidestep beyond the snake

Don't listen to his evil hiss

Be wise, love, and find peace

God is calling

The path is always there

The Windows Of Life

"There is a Monster under my bed!"

When I was a very, very, young boy

There was a monster under my bed

Well so I thought

It was down there with the dust bunnies

Just waiting for me

Fear came, so I pulled up the covers tight

Blankets over my head

This was my safety zone

As I grew a bit older, I learned the words to a song

Jesus Loves me

Jesus, yes, he would keep the monster away

But I grew older the monster was no longer under my bed

He was still there

Just inside my head

That monster has followed me all through this life

I have had him in backpacks

Saddle bags

Back pockets

Suitcases

Mike Kelley

Riding shotgun in my car

The monster haunted me in many ways

It was Southern California that I felt the ground shake

It was around the coast of Cape Horn a Typhoon

It was the monsoons in South-East Asia

It was a darken highway outside Bad Axe, Michigan

The curve not taken. the monster came

I watched the smoke lift

As my house burned down in Louisville, Kentucky

That monster came so many times

I have been cut, burned, shot, and beaten

The winds blew the day that swept seven states

Breaking down homes, and lives

There has been snow so deep

I awoke outside Flagstaff, Arizona almost buried

Outside Desert Palm Springs it was a sandstorm

Though blacken nights, and screaming storms

The monster came

He followed me as I worked my way breaking rules

The commandments of God, one by one

I allowed him to show me all the wrong paths

The Windows Of Life

I was in a world spinning out of control

In the South China Sea, I lost my best friend

He took his own life, listening to the monster

The monster took me far from home

It was a dream he painted

I wasn't there when my father passed

I wasn't there when my mother too

I listened to the monster all too long

In Cincinnati, Ohio my wife fell to a disease

Her life was threatened by Crohn's

The monster was back

Operations upon operations

Insurance lost, and our home taken away

The monster laughed

Then came the great Pandemic

I lost my employment

I lost all income and stability

My health taking a wrong turn

But, Halleluiah, I lost the monster

God had been in the shadows all along

He had a purpose for me

Mike Kelley

He awoke me in the night

Not like the monster under the bed

His voice spoke with understanding

I cried, and listened

He took away again my sins

We talked of purpose and direction

He gave me a pencil and his words

He restored me and my wife to a closer walk with him

The monster is gone

We face many things yet

We live in isolation due to the sickness of Covid

The world has changed around us

Yet, in all this we grew stronger though God's hand

He put light in our life

He put hope in our tomorrow

He puts his words each day in our study of the bible

He gave us a church we attend via video

A ministry of revival in Springdale, Ohio

He opened doors that the monster nailed shut

He is blessing us in so many ways

The Windows Of Life

Now we sleep in peace

There is no monster under the bed

Mike Kelley

Lift a Prayer of Peace

In a world of troubles

Lift a prayer of peace

Talk with God who spins us through space

It is his creation

lift a prayer of peace

Remove your boots, and lay down your toils

Lift a prayer of peace

Forgive others, and yourself to that Greater Spirit

Lift a prayer of peace

In this life so darken with evil

Lift a prayer of peace

Offer your soul to him above

Lift a prayer of peace

Tonight, before you go to your rest

Lift a prayer of peace

Then like the little dog asleep find peace

In yourself, and give of it to others

Lift a prayer of peace

The Windows Of Life

O' God of Christmas

You who gave word to Isaiah
He listened
He foretold of a child
(Isaiah 9-6)
His words called him, "Wonderful Counselor"
Then added he more, calling him, "Prince of Peace"
He foretold to a world of a peace with no end
In his shadow long past he spoke

O' God of Christmas where is the ear of mankind
Is it in lights of color on a tree?
Is it on the lawns flashing in December darkness?
Is it from a wreath upon a door?
Does the message get lost in ribbons and bows?
Has White Christmas taken away the light of Christmas?

O' God of Christmas, let us fall to our knees, as did the shepherds
We need not go to Bethlehem, or follow a star
We need you, O' God of Christmas
The angels singing once, sing again
Look down to the hearts of the Christian
Look down also to those who have turned away
Look down on a world of hate and darkness
Look down on us with you burning hand of love
You gave the world a son

Mike Kelley

You gave the world your son
The world rejected him in its darkest hour
Yet you left a printed path to follow
One though the pages, of your holy book
Once a Christ was born on such a holy night
There were no Jingle Bells, the bells that rang were of heaven
Yes, a manger, a lowly place, and a baby boy was born

O' God of Christmas open our eyes
Sickness spreads, across the world
Hate and fighting too
Mankind paints a holiday in red and green
But you, O' God of Christmas you paint the colors of peace
Peace beyond this world, beyond this life
Peace as foretold from your book of words
Not from the pages of some fantasy story

O' God of Christmas, how we have failed in your service
How we have failed in your callings
How we have failed and brought you down to our level
You whom we should lift up to
You whom above all gives hope, joy, love, and peace

O' God of Christmas, forgive us
Now bless this season of remembrance
Take away the lust for this world
Plant us in the dust of a mangers floor

To the unfolding of the true Christmas story

O' God of Christmas, let the angels sing, and the bells of heaven ring, and this Christmas hold us warmly as a child wrapped in swaddling clothes. Let us sing to you with our best and joyful voices.

O' God of Christmas, this now is my prayer lifted in celebration
A-Men

Mike Kelley

A Valentine

I made a few homemade valentines

Pasted hearts

Words printed across the front

Some I forgot to sign

Tonight, I am thinking of one

Crafted brightly in colors

Words written boldly

Rose are red

Violets are blue

Won't your please love me

For I first loved you

Jesus

Dreams

The Magic of The Mind
They Come to us All
Rich, Poor, Young, Old
A Vision of something Beyond
The Sweet Sleep
A Vision of Goodness
That Soft Touch we almost feel
Smiles found in the Heart
Dreams of Life
Birthday Dreams
Valentines Dreams
Christmas Dreams
Dreams of Tomorrows
Dreams of Hope
Dreams to make us Better
Dreams of Love Dreams of Sharing
Hold fast to your Dreams
Don't let the world hold you back
See the Colors
The Beauty
The Joy
Remember old Dreams
Plant Seeds of New
Dream with a Prayer
Let go of Fear
Embrace the Darkness with Dreams
These are the gifts of the Angels
Given to the Magic of the Mind

Mike Kelley

The World Has Outgrown Me

Seems I don't fit anymore
Old school thinking has no place today
People don't shake your hand and look into your eyes
Real friends are hard to find
People you could just talk with on the front porch
Special times were when family away came home
The State Fair had a rodeo
The drugstore had an ice cream counter
A kiss could change your life
Downtown was an adventure
Sears was a book of wishes
Furniture lasted a lifetime
Every home had a photo album with a story in every picture
Grand Parents weren't put into old folks' housings
Books were a treasure with each page turned
The family bible was always at hand
Saturday night was bath night
Sunday was church day
A mailbox sat on a post with handwritten letters
You knew all your neighbors by name and their families
If someone was in need you helped as best you could
Swear words would get your mouth washed out with Ivory soap
Now it seems swear words are in too many songs
Kids don't shoot marbles anymore or play jacks
Country roads aren't dirt anymore

The Windows Of Life

Clothes and shoes were for a year
Christmas was not X-mas
Easter was a time to recall its meaning
Holidays were times with family to share
Air conditioning was an open window with a screen
The sounds of whip-poor-wills brought a smile
A treasure was finding an arrowhead and wondering its history
The American flag was in every classroom and a pledge to it spoken
The President was a man everyone trusted and could believe
Farmers were people with names, not corporations
A service station was just that, and a face of a person you knew
Homemade things were always special, made with love
Postcards were treasures in the mail with a story to tell
Life and Look were magazines that become well worn by all
There were clotheslines that gave that special outside smell to clean
Ice cold watermelons on a hot summer day under a shade tree
Any open field could become a softball game at anytime
Horseshoe pitching would make someone shout "Ringer"
Then a prayer called for everyone to say A-men and mean it

Clouds of white changing shape were wonderlands of dreams
Blackberry cobbler hot with ice cream cold still makes me smile
The sparkle of the morning dew on a spider's web was a work of art
Cold mornings with hot cocoa and oatmeal around the breakfast table
There was a time a pocketknife wasn't a weapon it was a tool
Watches and clocks had to be hand wound
Ink pens didn't have ballpoints
Pencil sharpeners were hand cranks
School tablets were "Big Chief" with a picture of a Native American on the cover
We were one nation under God, and in God we trust
Valentines were given with thought and love to someone special and most handmade
The radio had tubes that would light up and bring us moments of entertainment with programs like, "The Shadow" or "Lights Out" or on the lighter side "Little Orphan Anne"
Music from the Grand O Opera, WSM out of Nashville, Tennessee
I still sing 16 Tons, as Tennessee Ernie Ford did
Skeeter Davis from Dry Ridge, Kentucky became a music star, and Kitty Wells had a real country voice.
Baseball games you could afford to go to without taking out a loan and the hot dogs were the best

The Windows Of Life

Shoot-outs were the bad guys and good guys, Roy
Rogers, The Lone Ranger, and the Cisco Kid, all would
win out over evil on Saturday mornings
For the world beyond was, Flash Gordon, The Green
Lantern, and Superman
Things just aren't that way anymore
What was make believe is gone
No more Peter Pan and Captain Hook
No more Tom Sawyer and Huck Finn
History has put them to rest
No, I just live in a world that has outgrown me
I won't have a tale to tell any kid as they are too dull
What was is gone
I wonder if God ever looks down on us and remembers
life as it used to be
Back in the days of Adam and Eve
Back when Noah was on the waters
Moses heading for that promised land
Back when this world took away his son
He must feel as I do now
The world is outgrowing him too.
Yet we hold on,
There is always hope for a new tomorrow
Maybe an old dog, a horse, and a little land to ride
And I see the sunset with a campfire and prayer
Then as a new day comes, it will be coffee with the
Lord
That is one thing that hasn't outgrown me

Country Mail

Cold and wet was my walk
Mud deep on my boots
Down past the fence
Took the old dog along too
We scared up a rabbit along the way
Wind blew with a mist in the air
People don't much write these days I guess
Yet maybe today I might find a letter
It has been such a long time
Just praying you are OK
Gone as you must from these fields
Gone from this off-road life
There is a light in the window for you at night
If ever you come back this way
Coffee is always hot too
Sure, would love to sit and talk over a cup
The paper calls for a cold winter this year
Sure, hope that is wrong
The barn needs a little work yet
But the roof is ready
Down at the crossroads they put up a new railway crossing
Sure, is a sight to watch the Norfolk and Southern go by
You know at nighttime dark how we would watch the stars
Well, I miss that and your hand in mine

The Windows Of Life

Uncle Billy came by with a new pick up too shiny for me
He has a job at the mill and doing OK he tells
Put your picture in a new frame and hung it over the fireplace
Looks right nice too with the glow at night
Heard WSM on the radio playing that old song
Hank was singing I guess he is lonesome too
Down at the church house they got a new minister
Young man with a good talking voice
Boyd's creek had beavers that built a dam
Flooded back past the bottom land
Laughed you would at the fish in the hay field
Old dogs got a limp these days
Don't take him out to the upper woods anymore
I was up to the sycamore you know the one I carved our names in
Would you believe I found my pocketknife there after all these years?
Well, it is getting late, and my pencil lead is about used up
I'll send this letter to you just to let you know things
The rain has let up some
So, I'll get off to the mailbox
Sure, would like to find a letter from you
Wish for it every day
Take care and if you don't write back that's OK
Just think about me sometimes
You always have a home to come too
Sure, would love to see you here come Thanksgiving
Love you, Lifting prayers for you always

Mike Kelley

Fall is Fading

The colors too
Mellow coolness, now cold
Sunlight falls as rays through grey clouds
Blooms are lost laying as lifeless petals
Bees hum no more
Butterflies lost from view
Days shorten of light
The calendar marks winters approach
A smell of woodfires lift from chimneys
Frost lays over the long grasses
Darker days bring candles to windows
Even that old moon hides its light
The sleep of nature has arrived
There is a slowness to life
Prayer lifted by the bedside
Soon we will rest under a grandmother's quilt
Our dreams will be of a new spring
All this as, fall is fading

Thanksgiving Prayer

Hello God, It's Me Again
Lifting a Thanksgiving prayer
Thanks for your blessings in this life
For a place called home
For the woman who puts a candle in the window
For the warmth of love around me
This land filled with all its wonders
For the family I love, those here and beyond
For a good horse and dog
For the sound of church bells that still ring
Thanks for this country, even with problems at times
Thanks for good neighbors with their smiles of friendship
And thanks that is not about a great feast, but the meaning
If it is bread, I break let it be with you
If it is a cup, let that also be with you
My Thanksgiving is beyond more than a day
Beyond more than this life
My Thanksgiving prayer is lifted to you Lord
For Jesus and his Thanksgiving to this world
If rain comes to the land
If there is lightning and thunder
If clouds seem endless
If the winds rip
If sickness is all about
If evil seems greater than good

Mike Kelley

If darkness seems to linger
I will be thankful for you Lord
This is not the end of our trails
There is a place of welcome, beyond this life
A place where the Angels give thanks
A place where the souls of your hands with gather
A place of the Greater Thanksgiving
Till we are called from this life
It will be my mission to tell of that Greater
Thanksgiving
I will sing it to everyone who will listen
From the campfire prayers your name will be spoken
So as Thanksgiving comes to the earth
Let it come with as much peace as mankind will allow
Let it come with your blessing to your chosen
Let it come from my house to yours
Let that candle my woman has lit shine in the window
of heaven
Let there be peace on this earth and goodwill
worldwide
Let there be faith restored in those who have slipped
Open the doors of the heart of men and women
everywhere
Help us to feed those without
To help our brothers and sisters in need
Keep our minds pure and let us be a reflection of you
This is my Thanksgiving prayer
Thanking you for your blessings given
Thanking you for a trail home
A-Men

Old, Faded Photo

Hello God, It's Me Again
Tonight, I sit and recall
It is an old, faded photo
But the place is clear to my mind
Here one can look out to the lands below
This place is called "Shawnee Lookout"
How tonight I would love to ride again
Take old Paint to the upper tree line
Make camp and view the sight
Sit with my dog Rope close by
Feel the peace with you Lord
Just a small campfire to light the night
Here to pull free my bible from the saddlebag
I would read the story of you Jesus
The words from that place called Gethsemane
It was in the book of Matthew that records it
In chapter 26 verse 36 it was here you lifted prayers
I too would lift prayers in remembrance
I would not have disciples, just my horse, and dog
Yet prayers would lift above the smoke of the campfire
Prayers up thought the night past the stars above
Prayer that recalls your sorrow
The Angels came to you as your earthly end was so near
I will cry in the night
Jesus, I would worship you in that high place
Below the waters of a great river flow here
It was the rivers of life to the early settlers

Mike Kelley

That river divides Ohio, Indiana, and Kentucky in view
As the night passes and the sun finds day
I would cinch up a saddle and follow a deer path
For it would lead to the water's edge
Rope would run ahead to clear the path
As farms lay below, I might hear the cock crow
It would be to Peter my mind would shift
How he denied you three times as the cock crowed
Tears may again fall from my eyes
I wonder how many times in my own way I denied you Jesus.
Forgive me Lord, for the spirit was willing but I was weak in the flesh
When I reach the lower level of the path
The place where the deer come to drink
I would recall other rivers
One that you Jesus was Baptized within
Pure from sin yet you were lifted up
You set an example for mankind
The cleansing of spirit washing of sin
Here by the water's edge new prayers would lift
And again, I would cry unashamed
For as you too cried my cry would be as free
You gave us parables, You, gave lessons in life, then you gave of you blood
I rejoice it didn't end on that old hill on a cross
I rejoice it was an empty tomb
I rejoice that you gave a life beyond this world
I may never see the Mount of Olives
No, never see that praying spot a Gethsemane

The Windows Of Life

The place of the Skull will be too sad to view
Yet, I will rejoice with you in a land beyond the skies
This is a prayer of tears and thanksgiving
Thanksgiving for all blessings giving
Thanksgiving for sins released

This prayer started from an old, faded photo
But what is not faded is you
Help me to paint your picture in other minds
Cast my words with the color of your life
Open hearts and eyes beyond this world
My boots may be covered in the mud of life
But it is "Holy Ground" as you come in spirit
It is time now more than ever to walk closer to you
Guide my steps in your trails   A-Men

Johnny Letter

The Letter
Within this darken night I linger restless
The fire in the hearth is but ambers
That roaring rush has departed
Just a line of yellow above the orange glow
Yet it cast shadows slowly dying to ashes
Long past the witching hour the clock works move
There within the mechanics counting time
The window allows a sliver of the moon a view
Sadly, it lays as clouds fade past leaving a veil of grey light
Out in the world beyond trees move with the breezes
Leaves of summer have turned to autumns colors
Shivering and losing grip of the mother tree
Taking flight across the fields to become a carpet of nature
Somewhere an owl calls out lurking for the field rodent
Tis a sad night beyond as seasons change
My eyes fall across the pages still wet with ink
Words dance upon the lines
The last few will be cast to the page
These indigo marks come with my last harvest
An inkwell cries for more ink
Yet, I cast to its holder, as the pen rests
The final signature made
Thoughts come from somewhere
Those voices of self
Voices asking without an answer, just asking

The Windows Of Life

Laughing, the fool has spoken not
Pondering life is for others, I am not God
The oak chair squeaks in recline of my weight
Casting feet to the desk with eyes closed
Hearing my heartbeat slow now
The breath too
Soon slumber will call
Yet now just a moment more in parting thoughts
On tomorrows post the letter will move
Across the lands it will move
Then before weekends next, she will open
Folds will be laid flat to her hands
Fingers will trace over the words
My mind will be exposed for what it is
The message will fill her eyes
Then the surprise will be to her heart
Tears may fall in early response
Holding the post close maybe to kiss the page
My Dearest Darling will ring to her ears
I will be with you to celebrate that Holy Day
Have your smile warmly awaiting
For I will be home for Christmas
This war calls me yet one more time
And whatever the outcome may be
I will be home for Christmas
If for reasons beyond myself
The world pulls at me
I will send my spirit and love
For death will not part
I will be home for Christmas
The letter arrived in the post

Mike Kelley

As a man in uniform knocked
While in service of his country
The letter cried
Thanksgiving passed as snow fell softly
Her heart broken she prayed to God
Not for herself but for an end to the evil of war
For hope of others awaiting loved ones
That they might be at the door and home
Snow fell as the calendar changed
Pure white it lay upon the earth
Memories passed of what might have been
Her window exposed a wonderland beyond
The pines of green holding fluffs of white
A cardinal upon the fence post
Children playing as snowmen came to life
Songs of the season playing on the radio
Then came the words
I'll be home for Christmas
And just then it happened
Through her tears she watched a man beyond
His arms loaded with holiday boxes
There was a big candy cane on top
He turned at the gate and approached
The bell rang
And there he was
Her Johnny did come marching home
And home for Christmas too
No, no one else saw her Johnny
But for one day that Christmas
She held on to his dream

His letter upon her tree.

For the world in which we now live with all the problems and trials, with all the bitter winds blowing in a world of hate, with all that is, be the one to come home for Christmas, for it is the day of hope that fills the Christian hearts, have faith in God, and celebrate with all your hearts even if it is only a letter upon someone's tree, be home for Christmas.

Jesus went to the cross and Johnny didn't come marching home, well, not to this world, but Jesus was lifted up and all the Johnnies of the world will be waiting for that Holy Homecoming.

Somewhere a mother and father, brother, and grandparents and loved ones have gone on to be held in holy hands. It would be my wish to pass on I will be home for Christmas to celebrate again that Holy Day and what a day it will be.

Mike Kelley

I Was the Arm That Held You

You shivered against my weight
Tears of loss burned from your eyes
Darkness I pushed away
You spoke of pain, and I listened
Every word whispered from a broken heart
In your limp hands you found mine holding
You wished for some other yesterday
One that now will remain locked in memory
Through the night we talked, you and I
The questions asked you already had the answers to
The night passed and the dawning of a new day came
You awoke from a broken sleep
Yet through the night I watched over you
Yesterday's pain will linger
Yesterday's tears will dry
 Today I point you to a new purpose
A path of hope in this day
Tears of loss too I have shed
Why I asked, but like you already knew the answer
They took me to that place
It was for you I went
But today I came back to be the arm you needed
The hands that held you through the loss
The ears to listen to your cries
And the love beyond this world
Of life on earth, we are only passing
This journey takes us to a new tomorrow

The Windows Of Life

I too had my yesterday
But that was my journey taken
For you I walked that path
Knowing the end to be just the beginning
Move forward my child
For I will be the arm that will hold you
Just lean on me
Lean on my everlasting arms- Jesus

Mike Kelley

Slipping From the Hands of Jesus

The winds of life were blowing
Dark clouds filled the sky
The lightning flashed around me
As the thunder told me why

The life I was now living
Was all but in vain
I was slipping from the hands of Jesus
And beginning to feel the pain

The rain from my heart was overflowing
My eyes could see not more
There was just a shadow of Jesus
Standing at my door

I was slipping from the hands of Jesus
When a voice came calling, please
He said I will forgive you
That brought me to my knees

I was so very sinful
In my backslidden way
But yet here stood Jesus
And again, I heard him say

I have a place for you
As for every man
Then he reached out to me

The Windows Of Life

And I felt the scar in his hand

How could I have been so foolish
To go my selfish way
To let sin overtake me
Just a little day by day

Then he spoke to me
As only God can do
He said my work on earth is over
But I have a job for you

Follow with your bible
And pray from your heart
I'll show the task before you
Go quickly now it's time to start

And when you find yourself falling
Don't stop your journey then
I'll be there right beside you
Till your work has found its end

Mike Kelley

Once We Laughed Together

In this life I have sailed too many seas
Sailed to too many ports
Have lost myself in distant fogs
Visions of drifting pasts
Faces flash in memory
Then just as fast disappear
Our acquaintances seem so brief
Once we laughed together in life
Now the bitter taste of tears lingers
So many lay under markers of what was
Today the sun rises, and Gods hands lifts me up
It is to his purpose now moving forward
Old friends will return again
Beyond these horizons.

Rainbows With Wings

Once upon a very special day
Winnie the Pooh Bear sat on a log
It was at the edge of his favorite sitting spot
It overlooked a field of wildflowers
He watched the butterflies dancing from bloom to bloom
Piglet, his best friend saw Pooh
Then Pooh turned to Piglet and spoke
"Aren't they wonderful Piglet?"
Piglet was puzzled and said, "what?"
Then Pooh answered him saying
"The Butterflies aren't they wonderful?"
And before Piglet spoke a word, Pooh spoke again
"The butterflies, they are rainbows with wings"

You see beauty is in the eye of the beholder, and how we view the colors, and the touches God has painted to nature, we must smile at a Pooh Bear who sees things in a very simple way.

Mike Kelley

When Will We Ever Learn?

The letter came today as the world turned outside her window
Each word was placed in ink across the page
That ink was cold and factual
Now comes the thoughts from within
Hope for a homecoming is lost
Such a distance, more than a world away
No need to make the cake to celebrate
The path home is lost
Time had parted them beyond return
It was another war, a battle, and loss
Sunlight reflects the words of the page
Yet before the mail was open, she knew
Tears will come soon
In service of your country seems no reward
A country that will never be touched as she
She hears the words in her mind
The words of a song
Where have all the young men gone?
They have gone to graveyards everyone
Oh, when will we ever learn?
When will we ever learn?
Beyond her window and beyond view
Eyes will look to see nothing
Now comes a memory of love
Their moments to only them
She closes her eye to see the dream again
A dream lost all so sadly

The Windows Of Life

Why is it always war?
Why is it always another life taken?
Where have all the young men gone?
Gone for solders everyone
When will we ever learn?
When will we ever learn?
She will fold the letter and place it in the family bible
There are others there too
Tears will kiss the pages
Tonight, after the sun is gone
When the darkness comes
Moonlight will reflect through her window
Prayers will lift up for peace
And God will listen to her heart
She will take the flowers from the fields
And lay them upon his place in the earth
Where have all the flowers gone?
Gone to graveyard everyone
Oh, when will they ever learn?
When will they ever learn?
In this world since the very beginning of time there have been wars, history records names, and we pray God will record souls. Time will turn, and fighting will again come it is a circle that turns. Turn, turn, turn, when will we ever learn?

Mike Kelley

Wonder As We Will

There will be storms in life
Clouds will cover blue skies
Winds will blow coldly
Rains and thunder scream with anger
Our travels pull us ever onward
We build walls for shelter
Holding back, yet we find tears
Safe, yet something is missing
Lost in life with the wolves at the door
Our travels have brought us to this place
We have prospered well, yet have an empty heart
Our minds lift to our roots
Those simple times
The place we called home
Dreams of life change
Our days became years
Years now a lifetime
We close our eyes in those memories
We see again those old friends
Just as before they are there
We hear the ringing of bells from the old church
The mailbox stands by the roadside
Inside there is a letter
To the family, it is written
Words scratched in pen in ink
A name signed and stained with tears
It is a letter from your own hand
Written long ago

The Windows Of Life

Just a few words it held
I'm coming home

Mike Kelley

Sand Water

That fresh hush from the ocean
The tide comes washing to shore
Footprints are taken as the water returns to the sea
Those steps of time now gone
Gone are the love letters too
Taken away, lost to the world

Sand Water
Where goes those footprints
Once planted in the sands of time
Does the sea hold them as a memory to recall?
Will Neptune laugh at what was there?
Lines written with love removed
Taken from the hearts that gave

Sand Water
I watched it leave with the sunrise
Golden and flowing from where it came
The seabird cried such a song sad to hear
Yes, gone with the water are the footprints
Gone are the love letters now erased
Smooth are the sands that await

Sand Water
It is like our lifetime it comes
Giving us a place leaving our marks
A path that leads us across a world of living
Our footprints displayed as we go

The Windows Of Life

Moments captured in hearts of love
Moved to a horizon beyond

Sand Water
We are just travelers in life
Building for a better tomorrow
Leaving behind old hopes and dreams
Moving towards something beyond
Something promised we pray
Baptized in a new beginning

Sand Water
It washed up on a new place
Beyond this world we see
All our path has taken us to this new beginning
Every step we etched in our life
We meet here that Greater Spirit
Sand water flowing to a holy shore

Mike Kelley

Nobodies God

I awake each day mostly before the sun arrives
In the darkness, I pray
Me
Nobody

I will little be known in this life
Oh, a few written words may be to a page
A page that will yellow in time
The ink that will fade
Our time is limited to years on this earth
We live by the numbers of mankind
In those numbers, I am Nobody
Never a #1 at anything
Nor do I wish to be
Life is an experience of travels
Not so much from place to place
But a trip from birth to its completion
I feed the birds that come to call on me
And watch the flowers in my garden grow
These are gifts from a Greater Spirit
Gifts noticed by me
Others will pass by and never understand
The simple pleasures in what is just beyond a window
I thank my God for them

Then there are the church bells the call to worship on Sunday
Ringing out for all to notice

The Windows Of Life

But even when they don't ring, I still hear that call
My home is not that built as a monument of success
It is a Sugar Shack of peace within
My holding of treasures are tokens of little value
Net worth is a banker's term
I find color in the rainbows of life
The music of rain on the roof
Beauty in the light of the moon with stars that glitter
I see beyond horizons to That Greater Spirit
Then rejoice that I am nobody
And thankful for my Nobodies God.

\

Mike Kelley

Let My Little Light Shine

Hello God, it's me again
I called to you and listened for your voice
Winds blew around the base of the mountain
I started to climb to get closer to you
Slipping and falling on my way
Each step on unsure rock
It was the rough side filled with danger
Climbing above your trees and grasses
Climbing into the clouds
Even above the birds
Oh, to be like Moses, to see the Promise land
My feet needed to be set on higher ground
Above the clouds into the cold mist
The day was passing
Sunlight kissing the day away
You knew I was coming
Holding for a moment the parting sun
Weakened at last I arrived
Cut and bleeding
My words lifted to your door
Hello God, it's me again
You gave me a mountain to climb
Broken and torn is this my lesson to learn?
To reach higher to follow your call
Night drew in as this universe lay exposed
Each star sending out light through the darkness
The moon itself reflecting what the sun gave
Here I stood on Holy Ground

The Windows Of Life

Bending to the rocky soil my prayer lifted
Calling to hear your voice
From the deep canyons below came an angel
One sent to open my mind
What is it you would have of me I asked?
The angel spoke telling me to open my eyes
Look beyond this mountain
Look into the skies
View the light of the moon itself
It reflects the light of the sun to the world
This is what you are to do
Reflect the light not of the sun, but the son
Reflect it to the world
You may at times climb other mountains
Climbing over the rough side
You may fall at times yet do not stop
Don't allow the foolish to sway you
Go now bring light
The light God will reflect though you
The light of the son
Now my friends if you see a Christian glowing
It is because they are reflecting
I have joined with them
Letting my little light shine

Mike Kelley

I Found Myself in Jesus

I found myself in Jesus
From my sins now I'm set free
He came to earth to save me
To die upon a tree
But the grave it could not hold him
Not no lock, no chain, no key
And with Love, he's here today

Climbing, falling, he will hold you
Praying, calling, he will hear you
Seeking, searching, he will show you
And with love, he's here today

I found myself in Jesus
From my sins now I'm set free
Do you know the way to heaven?
Won't you come along with me
Don't close your eyes to the savior
Open your heart now and see
For with Love, he's here today

Climbing, falling, he will hold you
Praying, calling, he will show you
Seeking, searching, he will show you
And with Love, he's here today

The above are the words I put to the tune of the Battle
Hymn of the Republic and sang it in a mission in

Phoenix, Arizonia years ago, with the homeless, the Navaho, and the hungry. Before that dinner hour was over it was sung several times. I don't know if it changed the lives of anyone, but it did open the night to a lot of folks asking questions while the answer was just a prayer away.

Mike Kelley

The Hope You Hang Your Hat On

Too many years have now passed

Years of fighting

Yet she holds out to the hope in her life

She, my wife has a hope

A sickness has brought her down

One doctor's say, there is no cure

Her body has been changed, yet she has hope

Faced each day with broken health, yet she has hope

The list of problems is long, yet she has hope

Her hope is lifted to God in prayer

Her hope is that the day will find some good

In dark moments carrying her cross she holds on with faith

She has faith and hope, like Job

Each night in prayers I pray for her, with faith and hope

Each day she fights when she falls, yet she has hope

God looks over her, her faith is stronger than ever before

We study each day his holy word

The Windows Of Life

Each day she opens her heart and soul to Jesus

We may not find in this life peace, yet she has hope

When the day comes, and God calls

She will be rewarded for her faith and hope

It was her words, the ones that make me proud

Words spoken for new tomorrows

Words that awaken her to hold on

She is the author of hope

She this woman of great faith

She this broken body

Her words inspire me

The first time she spoke it, I too was changed

When everything else is against, her faith and hope is stronger

Her words burn in me when she speaks them

Simple words, yet she speaks with faith

Hope to hang your hat on, she says

I lift my prayer with that same hope

Hello God, It's Me Again

Lifting a prayer for my wife

Lifting a prayer of thanks for her vision

Lifting a prayer for those moments of peace

Peace found in your hands

Listen to my prayer, Father God

Listen to her words of faith and hope

Hope to hang your hat on

A-Men

As you go through the travels of this book. If you have replies or thoughts, please feel free to express them.
mkelley1950s@hotmail.com

Other Publications by Author

For Everything and Everyone There is a Season: By Mike Kelley & Mona Hess, Parables Publishing, ISBN 978-1-954308-84-8

Hello God, It's Me Again: By Mike Kelley, Parables Publishing, ISBN 978-1-951497-02-6

It's Me Again, Hello God, It's Me Again
By: Mike Kelley, Parables Publishing, ISBN 978-1951497-32-3

A Christmas Trilogy: By Mike Kelley, Parables Publishing, ISBN 978-1-951497-77-4

In God's Hands, By Mike Kelley & Mona Hess, Parables Publishing, ISBN 978-1-951497-70-5

The River Cries: By Mike Kelley, Parables Publishing, ISBN 978-1-951497-93-4

Don't Listen to the Snakes: By Mike Kelley, available on Kindle.

Mike Kelley

In Conclusion, it was King David that introduced music into the worship of our God, sing to the heavens. May God, hold you close and let us rejoice together in his wonderous love, with song and music.

www.ingramcontent.com/pod-product-compliance
Lightning Source LLC
Chambersburg PA
CBHW030114240426
43673CB00002B/72